# OXFORD READIN

# ★ LITTLE BOOK ★

## OF

# POETRY

### *Chosen by John Foster*

## Contents

# Caribbean Counting Rhyme

One by one
one by one
waves are dancing
in the sun.

Two by two
two by two
seashells pink
and purply-blue.

Three by three
three by three
big boats
putting out to sea.

Four by four
four by four
children fishing
on the shore.

Five by five
five by five
little walking
fish arrive.

Six by six
six by six
pelicans
performing tricks.

Seven by seven
seven by seven
puffy clouds
patrolling heaven.

Eight by eight
eight by eight
fishes nibbling
juicy bait.

Nine by nine
nine by nine
taking home
a catch that's fine.

Ten by ten
ten by ten
tomorrow we
will come again.

*Pamela Mordecai*

# I Like

I like the taste of toothpaste
tingling on my tongue.

I like the smell of sausages
nuzzling at my nose.

I like the feel of sunshine
flickering on my face.

I like the sound of bells
echoing in my ears.

I like the sight of fairground lights
flashing in the dark.

*Moira Andrew*

# Seasons of Trees

In spring
The trees
Are a beautiful sight
Dressed in blossom
Pink and white.

In summer
The trees
Are full of treats
Apples and pears
And cherries to eat.

In autumn
The trees
Are red and gold
And the leaves fall down
As the days grow cold.

In winter
The trees
Are bare and plain
Waiting for spring
To dress them again.

*Julie Holder*

# The Garden Pond

There's something
In the garden pond:
A monster, huge and dark,
As slimy as a conger eel,
As hungry as a shark.

There's something
In the garden pond:
I've seen it roll and squirm,
All muddy, long and slippery
Like one enormous worm.

There's something
In the garden pond:
It's eaten all the fish,
If you go down the garden path
You'll see it splash and splish,

You'll hear its nasty slithering,
Its bubble and its fizz,
There's something
In the garden pond.
There is! There is! There is!

*Richard Edwards*

## Chinese Rain Dragon

Dance, Dragon, dance.
Make the rain come.
Dance, Dragon, dance.
Banish the sun.

Dance, Dragon, dance.
Beat on the drum.
Try, Dragon, try,
To make the rain come.

The earth is dry, Dragon.
Crops will die, Dragon.
Bring dark sky, Dragon.
Oh when will it come?

Try once again, Dragon.
Here comes the rain, Dragon!
You have won, Dragon.
Dragon! Well Done!

*Ann Bonner*

## Storm

The sky is full of dragon light.
The forks of lightning flash.
The sky is full of dragon roars.
The rolls of thunder crash.

The dark clouds race across the sky.
Down comes the pouring rain.
The green shoots burst out of the earth.
The farmer smiles again.

*John Foster*

# The Sea

The sea can be angry.
The sea can be rough.
The sea can be wild.
The sea can be tough.

The sea can rip.
The sea can tear.
The sea can roar
Like a hungry bear.

The sea can be gentle.
The sea can be flat.
The sea can be calm
As a sleeping cat.

The sea can glide
Over the sand,
Stroking the beach
Like a giant hand.

*John Foster*

## Left Out

It feels as if pins
Are pricking at my eyes.
My face is burning hot.
A firework is trying
To go off inside me.
My feet are glued to the spot.
My hands are rocks in my pockets.
I want to run away.
But my legs are rooted to the ground
Like trees. I have to stay
And listen
To everyone calling me names
And not letting me
Join in with their games.

*Celia Warren*

# Silverly

Silverly,
  Silverly,
Over the
  Trees
The moon drifts
  By on a
Runaway
  Breeze.

  Dozily,
    Dozily,
  Deep in her
    Bed,
  A little girl
    Dreams with the
  Moon in her
    Head.

*Dennis Lee*